WITHDRAWN

A Pattern Scavenger Hunt

by Kerry Dinmont

The Child's World®
childsworld.com

Published by The Child's World®
1980 Lookout Drive • Mankato, MN 56003-1705
800-599-READ • www.childsworld.com

Photographs ©: Shutterstock Images, cover (top left), cover (top middle), cover (middle left), cover (bottom right), 3 (top left), 3 (top middle), 3 (middle left), 3 (bottom right), 4 (right), 5, 6, 7 (top), 7 (bottom right), 9, 10, 15 (background), 15 (right foreground), 18, 19; Johanna Goodyear/Shutterstock Images, cover (top right), 3 (top right), 17 (left); Hurst Photo/Shutterstock Images, cover (bottom left), 3 (bottom left), 12; Annmarie Young/Shutterstock Images, 4 (left); Anan Kaewkhammul/Shutterstock Images, 7 (bottom left); Susan Schmitz/Shutterstock Images, 8; iStockphoto, 11, 20; Alexey Lesik/Shutterstock Images, 13; Samuel Borges Photography/Shutterstock Images, 14; Grigorita Ko/Shutterstock Images, 15 (left foreground); Filip Dokladal/Shutterstock Images, 16; Ivonne Wierink/Shutterstock Images, 17 (right); Joe Christensen/iStockphoto, 21

Design Elements ©: Shutterstock Images; Johanna Goodyear/Shutterstock Images; Hurst Photo/Shutterstock Images

ISBN 9781503823655
LCCN 2017944884

Printed in the United States of America
PA02361

About the Author

Kerry Dinmont is a children's book author who enjoys art and nature. She lives in Montana with her two Norwegian elkhounds.

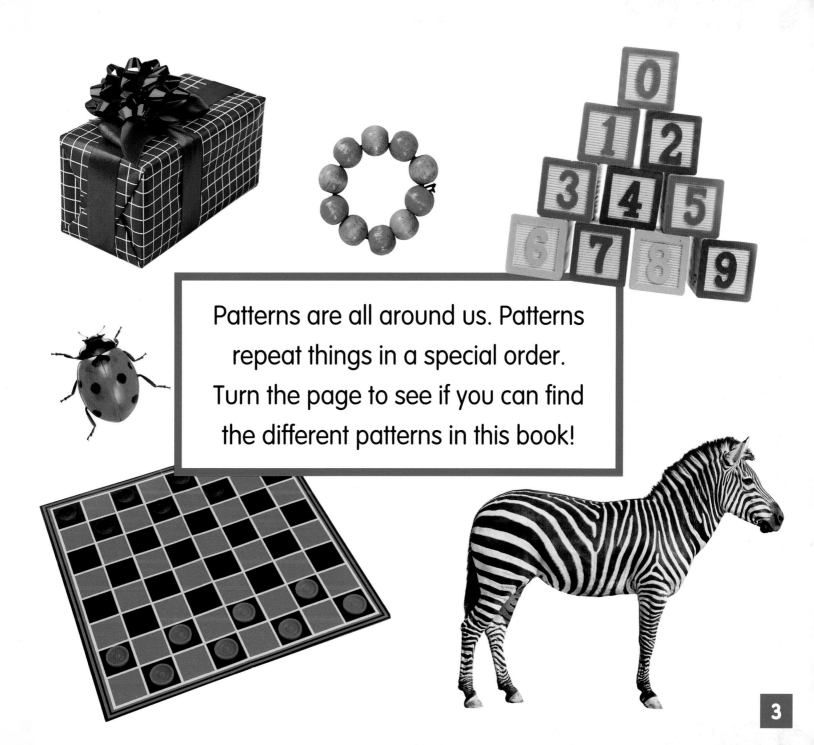

Patterns are all around us. Patterns repeat things in a special order. Turn the page to see if you can find the different patterns in this book!

Some patterns use groups of things. These groups can be colors, numbers, or other kinds of **categories**. Groups may be given letters. Group A might be the color red. Group B might be the color pink.

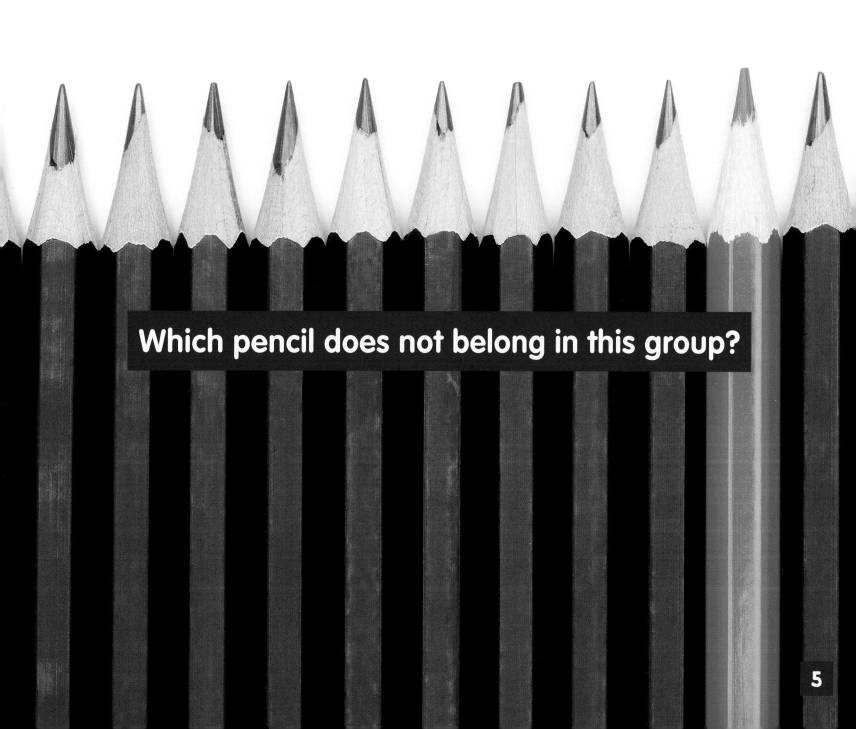

Which pencil does not belong in this group?

5

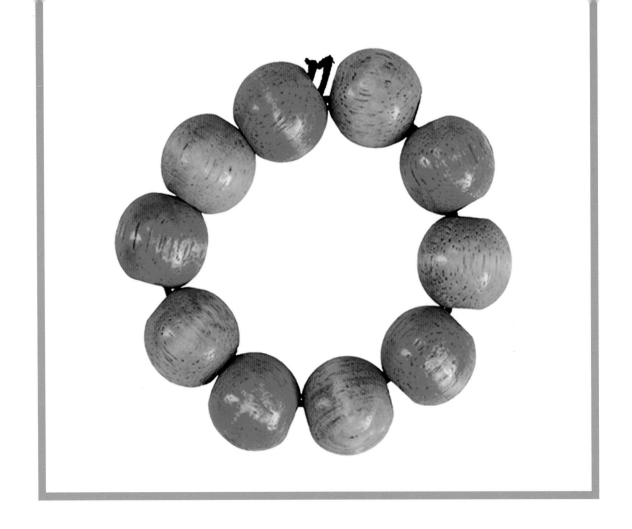

A simple pattern is group A, then group B, then group A, then group B. This is an ABAB pattern. An ABAB color pattern could be: blue, green, blue, green. Animals can have ABAB color patterns.

Can you find the animal with the ABAB color pattern?

The ABCABC pattern uses three groups of things. It is **similar** to the ABAB pattern. But it adds one more group. An ABCABC color pattern could be: white, red, green, white, red, green.

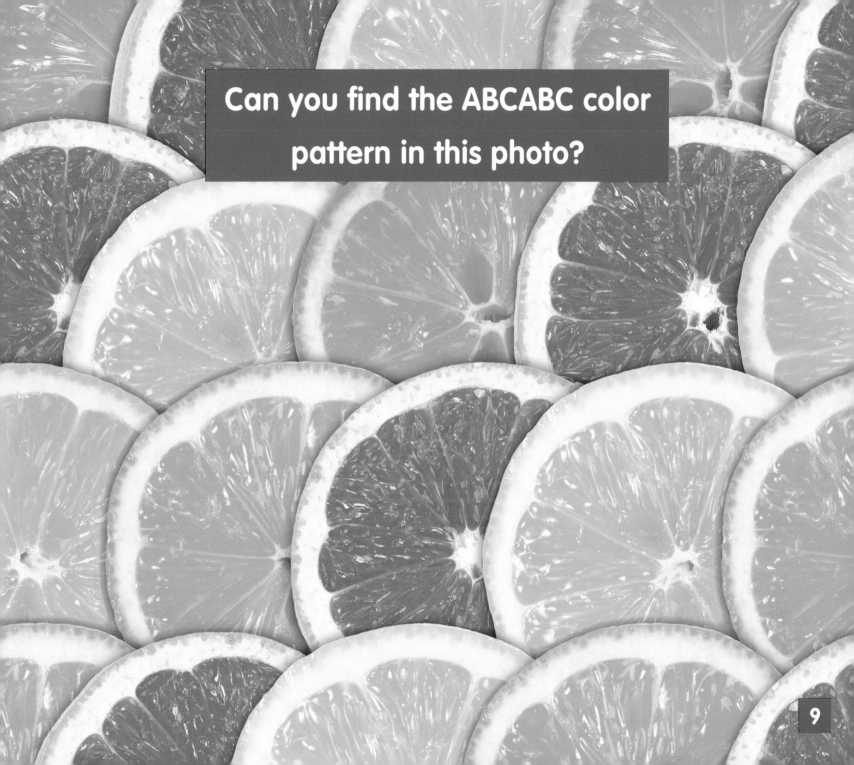

Can you find the ABCABC color pattern in this photo?

Patterns can help us **predict** what comes next.
We know that if a pattern is ABABA, the next item
is a B.

Which color Popsicle comes next in this pattern?

Some patterns cover a wide area. A checkerboard is like a square ABAB pattern. Every other square is either red or black. Squares of the same color do not touch each other.

Which flag in this photo uses a checkered pattern?

Patterns can also involve words. **Rhymes** have certain patterns. A pair of words that rhymes can be grouped into one category. For example, a simple ABAB rhyming pattern could be:

My cat is **nice**. (Group A)

My cat is **fat**. (Group B)

My cat eats **mice**. (Group A)

I like my **cat**. (Group B)

Which rhyme has an ABAB pattern?

My dog is black.

His name is Ace.

Ace eats a snack.

Ace likes to race.

My dog is black.

He eats a snack.

His name is Ace.

Ace likes to race.

2 4 6 8 10

Numbers can make patterns. Two, four, six, eight, ten is a pattern. Each number increases by two. You can predict which number will come next.

Which group of numbers makes a pattern?

	1.	2.	3.	4.	6.	7.
Monday	Science	Music	English	Lunch	Math	Art
Tuesday	Science	Music	English	Lunch	Math	Art
Wednesday	Science	Music	English	Lunch	Math	Art
Thursday	Science	Music	English	Lunch	Math	Art
Friday	Science	Music	English	Lunch	Math	Art

Our daily **routines** have patterns. A class schedule is a pattern. The events, or classes, in a schedule happen in a certain order. The order might be: science, music, English, lunch, math, art. This order is the same every day.

Which class comes after lunch on this schedule?

	MONDAY	TUESDAY
8:00 am	Math	Math
9:00 am	English	English
10:00 am	History	History
11:00 am	Lunch	Lunch
12:00 pm	Science	Science
1:00 pm	Geography	Geography
2:00 pm	Music	Music

Patterns are everywhere. They are in things
we see, hear, and do.

What patterns can you find at the fair?

Answer Key

Page 5   **Which pencil does not belong in this group?** The red pencil does not belong in this group. All of the other pencils are black.

Page 7   Can you find the animal with the ABAB color pattern? The zebra has an ABAB color pattern.

Page 9   Can you find the ABCABC color pattern in this photo? The ABCABC color pattern in this photo is green, red, orange, green, red, orange.

Page 11   **Which color Popsicle comes next in this pattern?** A pink-colored Popsicle comes next in this pattern.

Page 13   Which flag in this photo uses a checkered pattern? The black-and-white flag uses a checkered pattern.

Page 15   **Which rhyme has an ABAB pattern?** The rhyme on the left-hand side of the page has an ABAB pattern.

Page 17   Which group of numbers makes a pattern? The group of numbers on the left makes a pattern.

Page 19   **Which class comes after lunch on this schedule?** Science class comes after lunch on this schedule.

Glossary

categories (KAT-uh-gor-eez) Categories are groups of things that have something in common. Patterns use categories of things.

predict (pree-DIKT) To predict something is to be able to tell what will happen before it has happened. Patterns help us predict what will come next.

rhymes **(RIYMZ)** Rhymes are words that have similar sounds. Rhymes have patterns.

routines (roo-TEENZ) Routines are habits or regular ways of doing things. Routines often have patterns.

similar **(SIM-uh-ler)** To be similar is to have something in common without being exactly alike. Some patterns are similar to other patterns.

To Learn More

Books

National Geographic Kids. *Look & Learn Patterns!* Washington, DC:
National Geographic, 2013.

Rebman, Nick. *Which One Is Not Like the Others? A Book about Differences.*
Mankato, MN: The Child's World, 2017.

Schuh, Mari. *The Crayola Patterns Book.* Minneapolis, MN: Lerner Publications, 2017.

Web Sites

Visit our Web site for links about patterns:
www.childsworld.com/links

Note to Parents, Teachers, and Librarians: We routinely verify our Web links to make sure
they are safe and active sites. So encourage your readers to check them out!